ABOUT

FRUIT

By Solveig Paulson Russell

Illustrated by Arnold Dobrin

Melmont Publishers, Inc
Chicago, Illinois

For Dorothy Rea

Also by Solveig Paulson Russell

ABOUT TREES FOR TOMORROW
ABOUT SAVING WILD LIFE FOR TOMORROW
NAVAHO LAND

Library of Congress Catalog Card Number 62-7005

Copyright © 1962 by Melmont Publishers, Incorporated, Chicago, Illinois

Lithographed in the United States of America

TABLE OF CONTENTS

Pages

4

WHAT IS FRUIT?

Fruit is that part of a plant that holds the seeds. Since most plants bear seeds of some kind, most plants bear fruit.

Some plants bear fruit we call nuts. But we do not think of nuts as fruit or eat them as fruit.

There are plant fruits that we eat as vegetables. Among them are cucumbers and tomatoes, squashes and pumpkins.

The fruit of some plants is used for things other than food. Thread and cloth, for example, are made from the fruit of the cotton plant.

This book is about some of the more common plant fruits we eat and think of as fruit.

Almost all such fruits are good when eaten fresh. Many make delicious jams, jellies, and preserves. Almost all may be canned to preserve them. Some are frozen, others dried to keep them from spoiling.

FRUIT FAMILIES

Fruits can be divided into three groups which we will call families. A fruit may be either a pome, a drupe, or a berry.

POMES Pomes are the core fruits. In all pomes the seeds are in a core in the pulp of the fruit.

Apples and pears are the best known pomes. Cut a pear or an apple in two. You will see that the seeds are in a core.

DRUPES Drupes are the stone fruits. In each drupe there is a single seed inside a hard, woody pit, usually called a stone. The flesh, or pulp, is all around the stone.

Peaches, apricots, plums, and cherries are all members of the drupe family.

Drupes are either clingstones or freestones. If the flesh clings to the stone, the drupe is said to be a clingstone. The drupe is called a freestone if the flesh does not cling to the stone.

POME

 DRUPE

BERRY

BERRIES Fruits that belong to the berry family are covered with skin or rind and have their seeds embedded in the soft pulp of the fruit. But berry seeds are not inside a stone or pit. That is the difference between a berry and a drupe.

Belonging to the berry family are the usual small fruits we think of as berries — the strawberries, the raspberries, the currants, and the gooseberries.

We do not think of oranges, lemons, and grapefruit as berries. But that is what the men who study plants call them because their seeds are embedded in the pulp of the fruit. These berries are often classed together as citrus fruits.

Because their seeds are in the pulp, melons are also members of the berry family. So are bananas. A date is a berry with a single seed.

8

POMES

Now let's take a look at some of the pomes, those fruits whose seeds are in a core in the pulp of the fruit.

APPLES Perhaps the best known pome is the apple. Apple trees grow in many places throughout the world. Today they are found growing in all parts of our country, but they did not always grow here. Apple seeds were brought over by the first white settlers.

The Indians were given apple seeds. And so it happened that apple trees were planted all across our land even before the white man moved westward.

You may have heard of Johnny Appleseed. His real name was John Chapman. In early days, as he journeyed about our country, he carried apple seeds and planted them wherever he went.

All apples do not taste the same. Some are sweet, some tart or sour. Nor do apples look just alike. Some have red skins; some yellow, some green. The skin of others is streaked with red or green or yellow.

The kinds of apples have been given names. You may have heard some of them — Baldwin, Northern Spy, Jonathan, Delicious, McIntosh. Next time you go to the market, look for apples with still other names.

Apples do not spoil as quickly as many fruits. They can be kept in cold storage so are found in markets all the year around. Their juice is often canned. It is also made into cider and some kinds of vinegar. Apple sauce is known to all of us.

Crab apples are small apples usually sour or tart to the taste. They are not very good to eat raw, but they make good jelly and pickles.

KINDS OF APPLES

KINDS OF PEARS

PEARS   Like apples, pears are pomes because their seeds are found in a core.

The early settlers brought pear seeds as well as apple seeds to America with them. Today pear trees may be found in most parts of the country.

Just as there are different kinds of apples, so there are different kinds of pears. Each has been given a name. There are Bosc pears, Comice, Seckel, and Anjou pears. You may know still others.

Bartlett pears are among the best known. Most of them come from California, Oregon and Washington. These western pears are large, juicy, and sweet. They are picked while still hard, when their skin is brownish-green, and are put in a cool, dark place to ripen. As their skin turns yellow, the flesh becomes soft and juicy.

DRUPES

Drupes, we learned, are the stone fruits. In each there is a seed inside a hard, woody pit called a stone. A drupe is either a clingstone or a freestone depending upon whether or not the pulp clings to the stone.

PEACHES The Spaniards first brought peaches to America. When these early settlers came north from Mexico, they taught the California Indians to plant peach orchards. This was before white men landed on the eastern coast of North America.

Peaches grow best where the winters are not too cold. They are raised in the Pacific Coast states and along the Atlantic coast from Massachusetts to Georgia. Ohio and Michigan also produce many peaches for the market.

Some peaches have yellow pulp, others have white. The skin may be yellow or pale green. It is often streaked with red and may be covered with a soft fuzz.

Peaches bruise easily when ripe because they are very soft. They must therefore be handled with great care.

Like pears and apples, peaches have been given names. So there are Hale, Elberta, Muir, and Elberta peaches. Can you name still others?

A peach that is not too well known is the nectarine. Because it has a smooth skin, it looks more like a large plum than a peach.

APRICOTS   The Spaniards brought apricots as well as peaches to the New World with them. They planted apricot trees in both Mexico and California. Today, California raises most of the apricots grown in the United States, though some also come from Oregon, Utah, and Washington.

Apricots are freestone drupes that belong to the peach family. They are smaller than most peaches. When ripe they are a golden yellow.

Because they are tender and spoil easily, fresh, ripe apricots are hard to ship from one part of the country to the other. They are very good when canned, dried, or made into preserves.

GREENGAGE

DAMSON

16

PLUMS   The early settlers found wild plums growing in America and soon discovered how good plum jam and jelly can be. Today plums are raised throughout the country.

Like peaches, plums are either clingstone or freestone drupes. Unlike most peaches, plums have a smooth skin.

The greengage plum has a greenish-yellow skin. The damson plum is small and dark purple in color. It is not good when eaten raw, but it makes delicious jam.

Did you know that the prunes you eat for breakfast are really large purple plums that have been dried and then cooked? Thousands of tons of dried prunes are eaten every year. Most of them are grown in the warm climate of California.

Prunes, before they are dried, are also eaten as a fresh fruit.

PRUNE

18

CHERRIES   Like so many fruits grown in our country today, cherries came to America with the early settlers.

These small, round, plump drupes can be divided into two main groups — sweet cherries and sour cherries.

Most of our sweet cherries grow west of the Rocky Mountains. They are usually eaten fresh, though they are also canned or made into flavoring syrups. Sweet cherries are sometimes candied, too.

Sour cherries, sometimes called pie cherries, are smaller and jucier than the sweet cherries. They are raised in most of our northern states, especially in those bordering on the Great Lakes.

Pie cherries are sometimes eaten fresh, but most of them are canned to be used later as sauce or in pies. Sour cherries also make good jam and preserves.

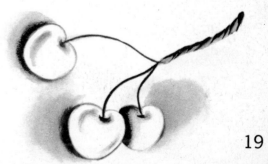

BERRIES

And now we come to the berries. There seem to be many more of them among the fruits than there are pomes or drupes. The berries, you remember, have their seeds embedded in the pulp of the fruit.

STRAWBERRIES A very well-known berry is the strawberry. Strawberries grow almost everywhere throughout our land. Because the vines on which they grow lie close to the ground, they were once known as earth berries.

The tiny yellow seeds of these juicy, red berries can be seen easily. They are in the pulp but very close to the outside of the berry.

We all know how good strawberries are when eaten fresh with sugar and cream. And is there anything that tastes better than strawberry shortcake? Now that strawberries are being frozen to keep them from spoiling, these delicious berries can be enjoyed the year round.

BRAMBLE BERRIES   Blackberries and raspberries together are known as bramble berries. This is probably because the vines or bushes on which they grow have so many sharp thorns or brambles. If you have ever picked these berries you probably found out just how prickly the stems of the plants are. They cling to anything that touches them.

Bramble berries were growing wild along the eastern coast when white men first came to our shores.

RASPBERRIES   There are two varieties of raspberries
— red and black. Black raspberries are sometimes
called black caps.

When raspberries ripen and become soft and juicy,
they can be slipped from their centers. This is because
the centers do not soften as the berries ripen. Perhaps
you have noticed that each raspberry is like a tiny,
plump bowl. The hollow in the middle of the berry
shows where it was fastened to the center stem.

Raspberries are eaten fresh and are made into jam
and jelly.

BLACKBERRIES   Just as there are two varieties of raspberries, there are two kinds of blackberries. One grows on thorny bushes; the other on thorny vines that trail over the ground. The trailing blackberries are sometimes called dewberries.

The centers of blackberries do not pull free from the outside of the berries as do the centers of raspberries. Instead, as blackberries ripen, their centers become soft. Next time you eat some blackberries, see if you can tell the difference between the taste of the outside and the center of these berries.

YOUNGBERRY

LOGANBERRY

BOYSENBERRY

YOUNGBERRIES, LOGANBERRIES, AND BOYSENBERRIES

During the last hundred years men have been working to grow better bramble berries. They have taken seed parts from one plant and made them grow with parts from another plant. This is called crossing plants.

By crossing bramble berry plants, three new berries were produced. They are the youngberry, the loganberry, and the boysenberry. They got their names from the men who worked to develop them.

CURRANTS Currants are bush fruits. They grow in clusters like grapes. They might be bright red, yellow-white, or black. The skin on these little round berries is shiny, which makes them look very pretty among the green leaves on the bushes.

Currants are sour to the taste even when ripe, but they do make delicious jelly.

GOOSEBERRIES Gooseberries are small, firm, green balls. They become soft and red as they ripen. However, when ripe they are not very good to eat, so they are picked while they are still green.

Gooseberries grow on thorny bushes. In fields where the berries are raised to sell, the pickers wear heavy gloves as they strip the bushes.

Like currants, gooseberries are much too sour to eat when fresh. They do make very good jam. And, if you have ever eaten gooseberry pie, you know how good that is.

BLUEBERRIES   Blueberries grow widely all over the world. Eskimos along the arctic coasts of America gather them. Boys and girls in many places in the United States and Canada go blueberrying in the summer time.

Many wild blueberries are picked and sold every year, but it is only in the United States and Canada that they are grown extensively as a crop. Within the past fifty years, men have found ways to grow larger and better blueberries.

One kind of blueberry plant grows close to the ground. The other is a high bush. The little dull blue balls grow in clusters. In order to grow well, blueberries need an acid soil.

CRANBERRIES   When the Pilgrims landed on our shores, they found wild cranberries growing here. Today these bright red berries are raised for the market. Most cranberries come from Massachusetts, New Jersey, Wisconsin, Washington, and Oregon.

Cranberries grow on low vines in marshy land. The fields in which they are raised are called cranberry bogs. The ground is flooded to keep it moist.

Workers use large, rake-like scoops to pull the cranberries from the vines. The berries are then sorted and cleaned before they are shipped. They are firm and do not spoil quickly, so it is not hard to ship cranberries from one part of the country to another.

Our main use of cranberries is for jelly and sauce. What would a Thanksgiving dinner be without cranberry jelly or cranberry sauce!

GRAPES   You probably never thought of grapes as berries. But that is what they are because their seeds are embedded in the pulp of the fruit.

More grapes are grown throughout the world than any other fruit. North America was a land of grapes when white men first came to its shores. Today grapes are raised all over our country, but the greatest number by far thrive in the California sun and in other states of the Southwest.

The fields in which the grapes are grown are called vineyards – a yard of vines. The grapes hang from the vines in bunches.

There are many different varieties of grapes. One that is well-known is the Concord grape. Concords are deep purple. Tokays are reddish in color. Thompson seedless grapes are yellow-green and so are lady fingers. There are red Malagas and white Malagas. Have you heard of grapes with still other names? Do you know different kinds when you see them?

Grapes are very good to eat fresh. Some kinds are made into raisins by drying them. Grape juice is used for drinking, for making wine, and for making jelly. Many grapes are kept in cold storage so that they may be sold in markets all through the year.

CITRUS FRUITS   There is one large group of fruits not often thought of as belonging to the berry family. It is made up of the oranges, the grapefruit, and the lemons.

These large, pulpy berries have thick, oily rinds or skins. They grow on low trees or shrubs. Citrus fruits need a warm climate. They cannot grow where there is much frost.

ORANGES   Less than one hundred years ago, to find an orange in one's Christmas stocking was a big treat. Now we eat an orange almost any time we choose. This is because so many more oranges are raised in this country today. They can be sent all over the country easily and they keep well in cold storage.

Florida and California produce most of our oranges, but many come from Texas, Arizona, Louisiana, and Mississippi.

There are two main varieties — the navel and the Valencia. The Valencia orange is smaller but it is sweeter and juicier than the navel orange. The nice thing about the navel orange is that it has no seeds. This makes it easier to eat.

Mandarins are Chinese oranges, reddish-yellow in color. They are much smaller than ordinary oranges and their skin peels off much more easily. Mandarins are sometimes called tangerines.

GRAPEFRUIT   A grapefruit looks like a very large, pale yellow orange. It certainly looks nothing like a grape even though it is called grapefruit. The name must have come from the fact that the fruit often grows in clusters the way grapes do. Some people also say that the flavor of grapefruit is somewhat like the flavor of some grapes. Do you think so?

It is only within the last hundred years that grapefruit has been eaten much in the United States. Now it is a common fruit on many breakfast tables.

Early grapefruit had a thick core and many seeds. Down through the years, men have improved this fruit so that we now have grapefruit that is almost seedless. There is even grapefruit whose pulp is a pretty, pale pink.

Florida leads in the growing of grapefruit. Arizona, California, and Texas also grow large amounts of this citrus fruit.

Besides being eaten fresh, grapefruit is canned. Its juice is both canned and frozen for drinking.

LEMONS On a hot summer day what could be better than a refreshing glass of ice-cold lemonade? The cool, sweet-sour taste seems to be just right.

Lemons are picked while they are still green. They are left to ripen in cold storage before they are shipped. This improves the flavor and keeps the fruit firm for shipping. Like oranges and grapefruit, lemons may be found in stores everywhere all through the year.

The juice of lemons is canned to preserve it. Lemon juice is also used in the manufacture of many of the soft drinks we buy. Frozen lemonade, too, can be bought in most stores and markets.

Look on the shelf where Mother keeps her flavoring extracts. You are almost sure to find there a bottle of lemon extract.

MELONS   Melons are among the largest fruits in the berry family. They need a long, warm growing season, but they are raised in many places all over the United States.

Most fruits grow on bushes or trees that bear fruit for a number of years. But the vines on which melons grow live only one season. Each year new melon seeds must be planted to produce new vines. The vines trail over the ground with the heavy fruit resting upon the ground.

There are different kinds of melons. Some, like the watermelon, are oval in shape. But most melons are big round balls. All have thick skins or rinds and a juicy pulp. The rind may be smooth or it may be coarse and rough. It may be yellow, green, gray-green, or almost white.

PERSIAN

HONEYDEW

CANTALOUPE

Sometimes the pulp is bright orange, as in cantaloupes, muskmelons, and Persian melons. Honeydew melons have a pale green pulp, while that of casabas is almost white. We all know the bright red pulp and black seeds of ripe watermelons. The seeds of the other melons are a light tan or a pale yellow. They are not embedded in the pulp as the seeds of the watermelon are.

Melons are best when eaten raw. They are never canned, though it is possible to buy frozen melon balls. The rind of some watermelons and cantaloupes is made into pickles and preserves.

BANANAS   What a strange berry a banana is! The long fingers, or bananas, grow in a bunch on a large stem. From fifty to over one hundred bananas may grow on one bunch.

A banana plant may be from fifteen to thirty feet high. Because it is so tall, it is often called a tree. But it is not a tree. The plant's true stem is under the ground.

Bananas are raised in hot, moist, tropical lands. Most of the bananas used in our country come from Central America, Colombia, and the West Indies. They are picked while still green and are shipped in refrigerated ships, trucks, and railroad cars to keep them from spoiling.

The bunches on the banana plant grow with the bananas pointing up. In stores the bunches are usually seen hanging upside down.

Some bananas look green even when they are ripe, but most of them change color as they ripen. Most bananas are yellow when ripe, though there are bananas with dark red skins.

Bananas are good to eat just as they come from the skin. They are also used in salads and desserts.

42

PINEAPPLES It does not seem that the pineapple could be classed as a berry, but it is. This is because each pineapple is made up of many small berries that have grown out from the stem to form one solid mass.

Like bananas, pineapples grow best in the warm tropics. Most of the pineapples used throughout the world come from Hawaii.

A pineapple has a tough, leathery skin that is full of deep, prickly dents. The fruit is very juicy and sweet when ripe. Only one pineapple grows on each stem.

While pineapples may be eaten fresh, most of them are canned. Before canning, the pulp is cut into slices or chunks, or else it is crushed. The juice of the pineapple is both canned and frozen. Frozen fresh pineapple chunks may also be found in most food stores today.

DATES   Even though it has but a single seed, a date is not classed as a drupe. It is a berry. This is because the date seed is embedded in the pulp of the fruit instead of being inside a stone or pit.

Dates are the fruit of one kind of palm tree. Date palms have a single stem or trunk. The feathery leaves and large bunches of dates grow at the very top of the tree. There may be as many as 1,000 dates in one bunch.

Dates grow only in a dry, hot climate. There are only a few places in the United States where they can be raised successfully. Most of the dates we use come from other countries with tropical climates.

When dried, dates can be shipped easily. They keep well for a long time.

FIGS   Most figs are somewhat pear-shaped. They grow on trees about the size of apple trees. They are raised in many countries throughout the world. In our own country, figs are raised in California and Texas. The trees are found also in home gardens in other parts of the South.

Some figs are dark, some are light in color. Mission figs are almost black when ripe. Smyrna figs are a pale green. Many people enjoy eating fresh figs. Figs are sometimes canned to preserve them, but most figs are dried. When dried, figs are either black or a dark brown. Smyrna figs are choice drying figs.

CONCLUSION

In this book you have read about some of our more common fruits. There are other fruits, many of them. Some you may already know. Others you will probably learn to know later.

Now that you have learned something about pomes and drupes and berries you will be able to look upon them with wiser eyes. Perhaps some day you will raise fruits to sell. Perhaps you will sell fruits in a store or a market. You may even study ways to improve fruit. Who knows?

INDEX

Solveig Paulson Russell was born in Utah but has spent most of her life in Oregon.

After graduating from the University of Oregon, she taught in both rural and city schools, for the most part in Salem, Oregon, where she now makes her home. Among her hobbies she includes photography, weaving, and wood carving.

Through her husband, an ardent outdoor man, Mrs. Russell became aware of the problem of the conservation of our natural resources. This led to the writing of **Trees for Tomorrow** and **About Saving Wild Life for Tomorrow** for Melmont. A teen-age daughter, Brenda, also has a keen enthusiasm for the out-of-doors, which has broadened Mrs. Russell's interest in the realm of nature.

Mrs. Russell has been contributing stories and verse to practically all of the magazines for boys and girls for more than twenty years.

Arnold Dobrin has studied art in California as well as abroad. Life as a free-lance artist has enabled him to combine travel with painting. Mr. Dobrin's paintings have been exhibited widely throughout the United States. He is a member of the California Water Color Society.